This book belongs to:

MIKA

Published by Ladybird Books Ltd
A Penguin Company
Penguin Books Ltd, 80 Strand, London WC2R 0RL, UK
Penguin Books Australia Ltd, Camberwell, Victoria, Australia
Penguin Books (NZ) Ltd, Cnr Airbourne and Rosedale Roads, Albany, Auckland, 1310, New Zealand

3 5 7 9 10 8 6 4 2

© LADYBIRD BOOKS MMIV

LADYBIRD and the device of a Ladybird are trademarks of Ladybird Books Ltd
All rights reserved. No part of this publication may be reproduced,
stored in a retrieval system, or transmitted in any form or by any means,
electronic, mechanical, photocopying, recording or otherwise,
without the prior consent of the copyright owner.

Printed in Italy

Stars and Planets

written by Lorraine Horsley
illustrated by Emma Brownjohn

When the sun goes down and night time comes, can you see millions of stars in the black sky?

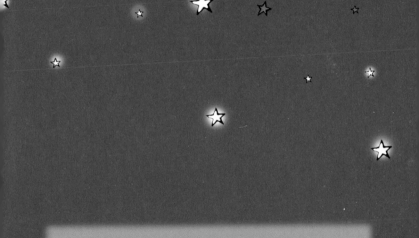

Stars are very big balls of hot burning gas. In space, some stars look blue and some stars look red.

Our sun is a star. The sun and all the planets that go around it make up the solar system.

Saturn

Uranus

Pluto

Neptune

Sun

Venus

Mercury

Mars

Earth

Jupiter

There are nine planets
in our solar system.

Here is the planet Mercury.
It is the planet closest to
the sun.
Mercury is a small dry
planet covered with
red rocks.

Mercury

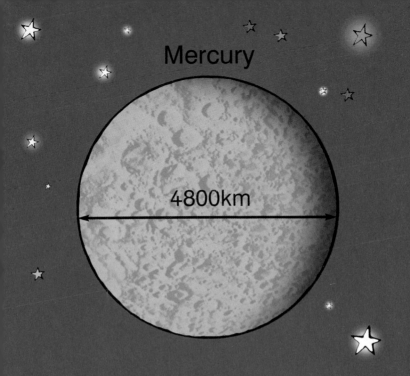

4800km

Mercury is covered with
many craters.
The biggest craters
on Mercury are about four
billion years old.

Here is the planet Venus.
It is the second planet
from the sun.
Venus is the hottest and
brightest planet in the
solar system.

Mercury

Venus

12100km

Venus does not have any moons.

Here is the planet Earth.
It is the third planet from
the sun.
Three-quarters of Earth
is covered in water.

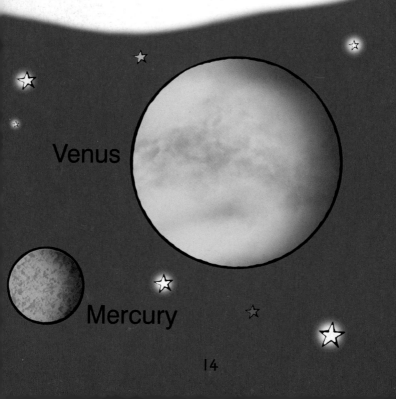

Venus

Mercury

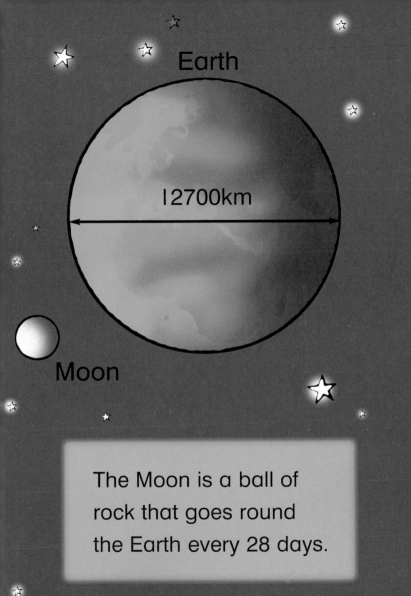

Earth

12700km

Moon

The Moon is a ball of
rock that goes round
the Earth every 28 days.

Here is the planet Mars.
It is the fourth planet from
the sun.
Mars is covered in red dust.

Earth

Moon

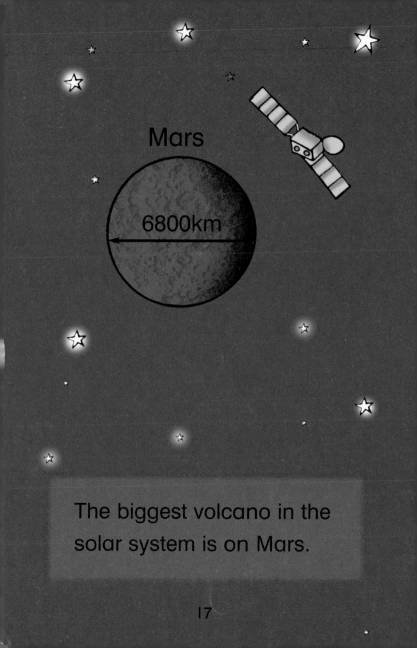

Mars

6800km

The biggest volcano in the solar system is on Mars.

Here is the planet Jupiter.
It is the fifth planet from
the sun.
Jupiter is the biggest
planet in the solar system.

Moon

Earth

Mars

Jupiter

143000km

Jupiter is made up of gases.
The big red spot on Jupiter
is a giant storm.

Here is the planet Saturn.
It is the sixth planet from
the sun.
Saturn has big rings
around it. The rings are
made of rock and ice.

Earth

Mars

Saturn

120500km

Three of Saturn's rings can be seen from Earth.

Here is the planet Uranus.
It is the seventh planet
from the sun.
Uranus is the only planet
to spin round on its side.

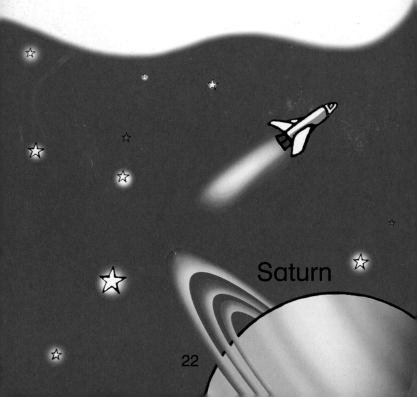

Saturn

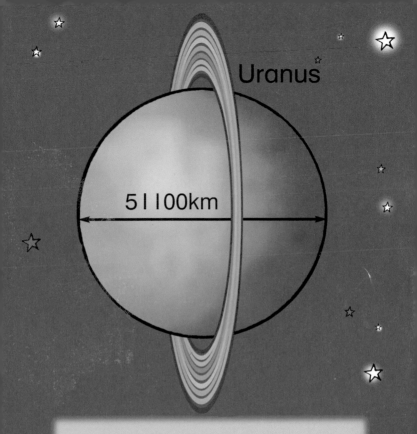

Uranus

51100km

It would take you eight and a half years to reach Uranus in a space rocket.

Here is the planet Neptune.
It is the eighth planet from
the sun.
Neptune has four rings
and eleven moons
around it.

Uranus

Neptune

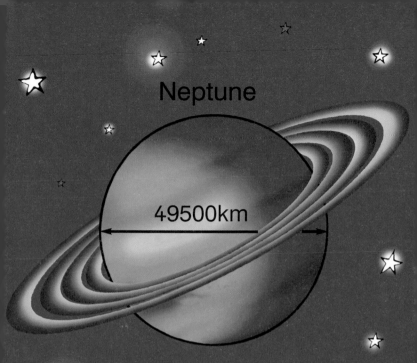

49500km

Space rockets can't land on
Neptune because Neptune
is made of gas.

Here is the planet Pluto.
It is the ninth planet from
the sun.
Pluto is the smallest
and coldest planet
in the solar system.

Neptune

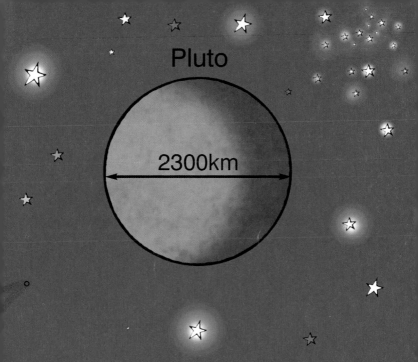

Pluto

2300km

We know less about Pluto than
any other planet.
It is so far away from the Earth
that no spacecraft has ever
been there.

Which planet would you like to go to?

Index